The Theory of Flesh

The Theory of Flesh

Poems by

Francine Witte

© 2019 Francine Witte. All rights reserved.
This material may not be reproduced in any form, published,
reprinted, recorded, performed, broadcast,
rewritten or redistributed without
the explicit permission of Francine Witte.
All such actions are strictly prohibited by law.

Cover design by Shay Culligan

ISBN: 978-1-950462-27-8

Kelsay Books Inc.

kelsaybooks.com

502 S 1040 E, A119
American Fork, Utah 84003

Acknowledgments

Grateful acknowledgment is made to the editors of the following journals, in which some of these poems were first published:

Blue Kettle Review, Blue Nib, Black Fox Review, Barbaric Yawp, Borski Press, Brevitas, Brine, Café Review, Cloudbank, Concho River Review, Descant, FLAPPERHOUSE, Fourth and Sycamore, Freshwater Review, Home Planet News, K'in, The Lake, The Long Islander, Walt's Corner, Midway Journal, Misfit Magazine, Panoply, Peacock Journal, Post (BLANK), Pski's Porch, Saranac Review, Schuylkill Review, Soft Cartel, Stoneboat, Thimblelit, Trailer Park Quarterly, Two Bridges Review.

A loving thank you to my husband, Mark, for his unwavering support of my writing.

A special thanks to George Wallace for his sharp editorial help on this manuscript.

And eternal thanks to Lori Schimmel Drucker, my sweet and darling sister, who lives now in Heaven. I miss you every day.

Contents

I

Evolution	13
How the Trouble Started	14
9 p.m., Somewhere Underwater	15
Meat	16
Guilt	17
Cave Dude	18
Bravado	19
The Theory of Flesh	20
Standing Shoeless by the Hudson	21
Dust Bowl Farmer, 1934	22
Someone Gets the Idea	23
Some Days	24
Morning, Turning into Day	25
I Look to the North	26
Some Nights	27
Moondot	28

II

When You Meet Someone	31
How to Make a Promise	32
Exactly How Many Me's are There?	33
A Stranger Shows Up, and He Looks Just Like You	34
Your Life Steps Aside	35
You Ask the Strangest Questions	36
What My Grandma Said	37
Questionnaire	38
I Am	39
So, When Michael Says Goodbye	40
Movie Theater, Last Showing	41
Breakthrough	42

The Night He Left Me for Another Woman	43
At the End of Us	44
What's Left	45
Here in the Hallway of Unfinished Love	46
Forgetting You Is Like a Lion	47
After the Movie	48
Bad Enough	49
How the Car was in Neutral	51
We Sit at the Corner Table	53

III

Something Dead Is Living Here	57
Sometimes the World	58
The Mosquitoes Show Up	59
Ownership	60
Anything…Something	61
How it Begins	62
Two Old Sisters	63
Grief	65
End of the Day	66
Doubt	67
Dogs Know	68
Cycle	69
Crop Failure	70
Instead	71
11:59	72
Thirst	73
Things I Didn't Expect	74

I

Evolution

First, the ape,
paw-digits poking
at sticks. Monkeybrain
seemed to want
a fire.

Later, early
man. Thin coat
of intelligence against
the cold. Someone stumbled,

flint against rock
and sparkshower tumbled
into the unlanguaged night.

Now, there's us.
Filthy with fires
and bloated with words.
We are scorched with war,
and we say nothing.

Future man
looks back on us
and shivers.

How the Trouble Started

First, the earth lifted its shoulders

    into mountains, then flat ground

went prickly with moss. The stars above

    buzzed electric in the nightcurtain.

The ocean licked the land, and that's

    when man crawled out, two-legged

fish with opposable thumbs, fashioning tools,

    touching everything he saw, looking

around for more when there was little left to do,

    his fingers starting to itch.

9 p.m., Somewhere Underwater

The fish night is beginning.
A whole world we don't care about
any more than they care about ours.

By morning, we will be baiting hooks
and flouncing nets. They seem oblivious,
dressed up in the fish finery—ruby tiaras

and strings of pearls they found
in a treasure chest. They dance among
the seaweed shimmy in the strobe

thrown down by the light of ships overhead.
And all of a sudden, Mayor Mackerel tailstruts
out, waving a fin to quiet the crowd.

Harrumph, he is saying in fishtalk,
we have to solve the problem of our young,
who every morning fall to the lure

of fat, tasty worms. We have failed to educate
them to the dangers of hookdangle and netswarm,
and the latest thing, this awful game they

play of getting caught on purpose
to see if they will be one of the lucky
ones that end up getting tossed back.

Meat

Next time you bite into a burger,
think about the last time someone
in your line carved flesh away
from an animal. Maybe it was

your grandfather, 100 times back,
greater than great. How his cave wife,
your 100 times grandma, had to set
a flatrock table, lay out bones that had

been fashioned into forks. Now, the hour
is late. Sun draining out of the sky. A rumble
in your grandfather's stomach and all he
can find is a baby rabbit. And, here it is—

food chain moment. The rabbit eye to eye
with your grandfather. It's been a hard winter.
Ice age closing in. Your grandmother's
back in the cave. She is rocking the baby who,

of course, will survive, or there wouldn't be you.
The baby will later fall asleep sucking
on a rabbit bone. Your grandfather will fill his own
stomach with snow and nod off sharpening

a stick that is still damp with rabbit blood.
The last thing he sees is his wife, huddled
in a corner, frozen rock, a table who won't
last the night, the fire next to her, going out,

with only a single spark still alive.

Guilt

A snake will slither up,
open its gallon mouth

and swallow a dog
in a single gulp like

it's a stick. And even
when the snake is full,

he looks around, his tail
flagged up, his stomach

big as a bucket, weighted
with a scoop of stones,

and in the air, the whisper
of *why are you just lying there?*

Cave Dude

had no craving for burritos, no need
of a board, no cowabunga here.
He was more concerned with the
oncoming ice age that might snip
off his fingerparts. Early each evening,

Cave Dude would go out for fire.
A regular at the local fire hut,
and once there, he would reach into his
pocket, his pocket a hollowed-out
mastodon ear, and fish out some
cash, the cash, an actual fish.

Then, he would trudge home over
crag and rock, back to his cave mom
and cave dad, who, like every other
night, were kneeling in the garden which
was glassed over with frost, the two
of them, arms raised into the icicle sky
which they were trying their best to forgive.

Bravado

Take away our medicines and guns,
and where are we, really? Not at the top
of the food chain, that's for sure. Our
teeth can barely tear a baguette, and forget
about breathing in the wrong stranger's
sneeze. Put us in the jungle, and watch
the tigers sniff us out. Nothing but
our bready hands to fight them off.
Tigers don't care about your negotiating
skills or your way with a presentation.
And bacteria? Small as they are, they are giant
to us. Salivating as they gather on the tip
of our thumbs. And us, armed only
with hand soap and woolen scarves,
while they just laugh and keep
lurking right there in the light.

The Theory of Flesh

states quite clearly
that the table of summer
is an open surface waiting
for you to speak your hunger.
It further states that it's up to you
to give your flesh what it's asking
for. Be lion. Be feral. This may
be your only summer. Go get it.
You're only abandoned if
you're waiting for someone
to come.

Standing Shoeless by the Hudson

She names the things that cover her
like cloth: work, love, maybe a latte

now and then. A fine mist shivers
as the sun goes from fist, to finger,

to gone. Minutes ago, she gave up her shoes
to an old homeless woman who turned

into questions—*how did this happen?* and
who were you once? The river, now in sunset

light, is skittery with fish and kayaks it soon
will forget. The evening cold comes on,

and her feet feel the sudden chill of what
goes unanswered. Meanwhile, everything moves,

keeps moving, like sunlight dropping into night.
like the river, which is also a ghost,

Dust Bowl Farmer, 1934

Back then, when the sky gave
nothing but wind and peeled the skin
plain off the earth, he just kept going.
Even as his life was falling in on itself
like a brushfire barn. He was determined
to be a man, like his father and his
father's father, too. Even when
his wife now took to secret drinking,
getting whatever she could from
the passing drifters and paying them
with her mouth. Maybe the rest
of the country, the bread-lined,
hat-holding, applecart lot of them,
didn't have to sink this low. Maybe
theirs was a glass that got filled
every now and again. No matter.
His thirst was constant, and it woke
him each morning at 3 a.m., made him
leave his wife in bed, drunken mountain.
Till this one night when he stumbles
out to the well and finds the last
of the milk cows fallen down dead.
No matter, he reasons, that's meat
for a week. But it won't be till later
that he finally gives up,
when he finds the fieldcorn kernels
dried into hard, little pearls. That's
when he stabs his hoe into the
earthcorpse under his feet, when
he curses the dry, gutless soil
for not even having
the sense enough to bleed.

Someone Gets the Idea

that if the bomb hits before lunch,
we scrunch up under our desks.
Which is cool during school, but
when summer comes, we are high
but not dry because humidity right?
No use splitting hairs, it's not the atom,
after all. If we are left to fend for ourselves,
so be it. But when we're in class,
the globe is one foot wide and spins
however we choose. The flag above the chalk
board, our mouths reciting the daily pledge,
our hands pressing faith into our hearts.

Some Days

all you want is to fit into the shape
of your shadow, stretched out
before you, nine feet long. No hint
of sickness, and death is what happens
to roses and other people. Those days,
you could go on forever, sun at your back.

And then, there are other days, your
shadow's behind you, shortened and squat,
clinging to your ankles. A funhouse
you that is fattened with every mistake
you'd like to forget. Those days,
you can't walk yourself out
of the you that is trailing behind.

Meanwhile, the sun hammers down,
trying its hardest to hit the street,
if only you weren't there to stop it.

Morning, Turning into Day

Time is tight, and you're out
the door, First stop, coffee shop
where you explain that you want

your eggs plain. Just the way you want
your life. No yellow eye staring
up at you. No one watching your

every move. You clean your plate
like your clear your browser history.
Certain it's gone. Your stomach full,

and the busboy stacks your dishes.
You pay the check, think this is over.
But halfway down the street, the taste

of breakfast is still on your lips, reminding
you of what you ate, reminding you, too,
that your search for love, for company,

is right now streaming out to the universe.

I Look to the North

where cold used to be guaranteed,
where the ice holds on, but only
for now. When I was a kid, the Arctic
was a long white page, unworded
and hushed. But now, each day the ice
splits, forming new coastlines, jagged
as bearteeth, opening to the blue surprise
of ocean underneath. My mother used to
say you needed change in order to grow.
And maybe the earth is turning adult,
and one day soon, it will be meeting
the other planets for coffee, all of them
heaving a sigh of relief about the rash
of humans the earth used to have.

Some Nights

you are an old man who, thinking
he once saved a jar of starlight,
believes that he can sprinkle it
anytime. You look at me, our love
gone like a daughter we lost
to disease, who now sits each night
at our dinner table and refuses
to be fed. We prop her up anyway
and coax silver spoons into her mouth.

I am an old woman who has
saved all of her dresses, convinced
they will come back in style. My
favorite a heartscarlet mini I wore
before we met. I have a photo of me
wearing it. I am a twist in a braid
of dancers on some ancient disco floor.

Most nights, I know I am not that
girl anymore, the girl who didn't know
that soon she would stop dancing, marry
a dreamless man and wear the same
faded dress forever. Other nights,
I nudge foodless air into our invisible
daughter, watch you walk away
from the table, listen to you
in the next room, trying to thunk
the starlight out of an empty jar.

Moondot

Late-night moon tucked away
in the sky, above the buildings

and struggling out of the clouds.
Small white eye peering down at us,

tiny dustmites with our own small
thoughts making us believe we are

planets. We are so much like that moon
tonight. An astronaut standing on

the bootstriped surface can wave
his arm into the neverending night,

but back on earth, he can hide
that same moon behind his own

held-up thumb. Little more than a morsel,
this moon, melting in the night's dark

belly. Small moon, small us
but really, the universe.

II

When You Meet Someone

You meet their whole life.
You meet their history, and now,

you are part of their next hello.
You meet the date who didn't

show up for prom, who left
them flowerless and silly,

or the butcher, who always
overcharged them for lamb,

and if only you knew that,
you'd understand why, for

a second, split as it is,
their pupils widen, animal-

like, as if you could be danger,
and maybe you are, you,

with your hand on
the snooze alarm, telling even

the day it will just have to wait
until you are ready to start.

How to Make a Promise

First of all, know it can break.
It is eggshell. It is the last frozen
lake of March, splintered and ice-
hollow, and crossing it will take
some risk. Add in words like if
and maybe. Throw in a detail
about your dying catmotherdog.
Nothing hospital. Nothing you want
to be true. As the promise day nears,
practice words like traffic and running
behind. Tell yourself you will learn
to be a better person. Remember
that this is a promise, too. If you
end up keeping your promise, buy
a bag of confetti and plan your own
parade. Puff out your chest as you
show up or call, or whatever it is
that you said you would do. Pretend
not to hear that almost silent sigh
of relief as the other person sits down
or answers the phone. Above all, remember
that they have just kept a promise, too.

Exactly How Many Me's are There?

There's the me in the checkout line
at the supermarket, ready with the debit
card. Moments ago, that was the me
who put the corn chips back on the shelf.
The same grown-up me who wakes me up each
morning and drags me to work. But there
are so many others. For example, the me who
is waiting to greet me as I get off the plane
if I ever make it to China. Or the movie theater me,
screenlight flickering on my face.
Then there's the me only my past
lovers saw. One by one, watching my
broken-heart face, sometimes a different
me watching theirs. Then there's the
facebookinstatwitter me. Emoji, emoji,
kitty-cat GIF. The posed, spontaneous selfies
I took a hundred times. Of course, there's the me
I showed my mother as I teenager-ed myself
away from her. The wifey me of my
first sad marriage. The me me me
of my sadder divorce. But here's the thing.
Tomorrow will bring yet another me
and after that, more of the same. And maybe
one day I'll stop counting, get the answer
to how many me's there actually are,
stop checking my reflection in the storefront glass
on the way to whatever me I'm about to become.

A Stranger Shows Up, and He Looks Just Like You

Dark eyes, like yours, dark with the end of us
just up ahead. I won't lie, I know he is you.

No cure for this sickness of desire that starts
and starts and stutters to a stop. Love

has a lifeline, blips and ticks and then plain
flat, beeping and over. The clock says noon,

hands straight up. Time for surrender. If this
were a western, we'd be gun to gun by now.

Mine would pop a silly flag, Bang, it would say.
Then, I would sulk off into a sunset sorry

under a told-you-so sky. The sky that watched
you walk into my life, waited until I was drained

of heat and color, then sucked me back into
the darkness, the same way it does every night

with the sun.

Your Life Steps Aside

to see what you'll do next,
holds its breath, holds the smell

of the paint on your walls, the fear
building in your sweat. Your life

knows what you dream about
and is quietly waiting, waiting

for you to hear the tick of the clock,
the spin of the wheels. You are used

to your life standing over there, tilting
its head like a curious dog. A part

of you wishes you had an answer
to give your life. The other part

shrugs it off, reasoning when
was your life ever *not* worried?

You Ask the Strangest Questions

Like what was the earth before
it was earth? You are torn between
science and God these days, believing
a little of both. God put the whole thing
in motion, you say, but then took his foot
off the gas. Let treematter form into forests,
and seacreatures form into man. Some kind
of nebula accident starting it all and *bang!*
there was the planet we are sitting on now.
Spinning us silly as we wait for our coffee

to cool. And here I am, sitting so patient as you
tell me you are going to go your separate
way. Later, I will think of this as the moment
I lost you. Even though I know how beginnings
start long before they begin. Endings, too.
Particles of love leaving the heart, invisible
to the naked eye. One less I love you, one

less touch. God and science all mixed up,
just like the forming of the earth. The end
of us is just another planet made up of one
small thing and then another until it
all collides, clutching itself into a fist.

What My Grandma Said

She told me life is an elevator,
and not because of the ups and downs,
the joke answer she would have loved,
but instead, she said, it's the way it closes
on you, sudden. No second chance.
Don't drift, she said. Don't end up
a collection of days, then years that
finally sprout wings that won't fly.
Maybe your memory goes or it's
the pain in your legs, and you are left
holding a handful of unplanted seeds
and wishing you had taken the elevator
up to the rooftop garden you heard
so much about, instead of breathing
the same old promises in and out
about a million times.

Questionnaire

You've been chosen to come up
with a definition of love.

Would you say it's A)
a golden road that begins

at mile 2,000 of your life?,
or B) where you put the dice

back in your pocket? Better yet,
C) is love that perfect moment

where dough rises into cake,
satin in your mouth, unlike

the sawdust you've been chewing?
Would you say that love is all

of the above? Or would you like
to write in a comment, say that love

is that ache banging around
in your chestcave, and you are

going to call the doctor
if it doesn't subside in a week.

I Am

then I meet you.
        Suddenly, I am
plural. We are, we are.
        No more lone star
shining its weak, streaky
        light on a cornfield
maze, no more sad dove
        wandering the sky.
Yes, once I am we, we
        quench our thirst
in the pool of together.
        Plant our seeds
in a lush brown field.
        It's a small thing,
this conjugation. I am,
        we are. Love
after all, coming down
        to a simple case
of grammar.

So, When Michael Says Goodbye

this time he means it.
No more calling you late night,
half-drunk and horny. No more
books or clothes he left
behind like bits of himself
in your brainteeth. This time
he's moved on. For real.
Met someone new and she doesn't
play. Doesn't buy the shit the others
did. Like you have a history or why
can't he have female friends.
This time when he unfollows
or unfriends you, you best believe
he's a ghost. And a real ghost,
this time. Not one of those clingy
ghosts that creak the floors or
tickle your ear or trip you on your
simple way from here to there or
anywhere you happen to be going.

Movie Theater, Last Showing

This late, the blinking light shines
back on the audience, and you
become the movie. You are the actor
who has been all Greta Garbo, all
Sean Penn or anyone else who ever
lived in public and wanted no one
to see. The light from the screen
holds you now in its sweaty palm
and squeezes out your secrets, the crush
you had on your brother's wife, how you
lunge-kissed her that Christmas. All of it
backstory now, and by the time the film
is over, and you reach for your coat, you
hope no one was watching after all, that
no one figured out how your story ends,
or thinks it is all too obvious, specifically
pointing to the scene with you sitting
all alone in the flickering dark.

Breakthrough

You are bad at family dinners, those cattle calls
of memories and walking ghosts. You'd much rather
live in the now. What you want to call your grown-up

life. Instead, you are sitting across from Uncle Max,
dead in five years, who keeps shaking his head
at your mother, his younger sister, who, herself,
will be gone in two. How they thought you'd be married

by now, or famous. And you are nowhere near either.
You butter your bread, your go-to move. No eye contact
needed, and besides, the food is good.

Later, the train will rumble you home, back to your
one-room life with its stack of magazines and people
you mean to get to. But listen, one thing at a time.

First, there is saying that today is the last day
of your childhood. And then, later, when you lie
down to sleep, be sure to close the curtain
on the moon staring at you through
the window like your mother's watching eye.

The Night He Left Me for Another Woman

looked like any other night. Black shade
of starless dark, the day draped over a chair.
He mumbled words like strong and change,
and right there I should have known. Should
have known from the way he walked around
and picked up photos, holding them a beat
too long. I told myself that distance is normal,
expected when you've been together this long.
I couldn't tell you the minute he took that first
step away from me, but I can tell you all about
the quiet click of the door closing shut behind
him, the gasp of the world outside, his future
without me, licking its lips.

At the End of Us

we drop our manners,
don't even stop for a proper
goodbye. Instead, we wander off
to all the places we would rather
be. We scale down to skeletons,
bare-boned, unhearted. The bodies
we were to each other lie rumpled
in a corner. We no longer need
them. Don't know them.
They look like the yesterday
that is just about start.

What's Left

is a room with a white-boned light
spilling through the window, sad
blue of the sea outside. And now,
the wooden chair that the husband
pushed back from the table. He told
the wife he was leaving, wanted to
be more like the sea. Nothing but freedom
and motion, the sparks of fish swirling
under the waterskin. And with that,
he slammed out the door. It will take
weeks before the wife can open the window,
let in the salt air, weeks before she can
cook a dinner of white potatoes
and unsweetened tea. She will know
that she has to live basic now.
One table, one chair, and one window
where she can finally look out
at the twist of waves, realize
that the sea is only moving, after all,
at the simple whim of the moon.

Here in the Hallway of Unfinished Love

Go ahead. Knock on the door.
You might not get an answer,
but if you do, press your ear close.
Linger a bit before grabbing the doorknob.
Stop for a moment. Notice your surroundings.
The hallway carpet, the floral design. The
management thought you would like to smell
the roses, if only the woven kind. Notice
the paintings, most likely purchased in bulk
at a conference room close to the airport.
Pictures of flowers, pictures of vases,
the kind your mother told you not to touch.
Think about the times a person even gets
flowers, first dates, and holidays, and then
again, when they die.

Inside, love is beginning to fidget. Let it.
Think some more about flowers.
About seeds and bees. Tell yourself that
the point of love is pollination, and you
are just a fancy bee who learned to tie his shoe.
Listen, love isn't going anywhere when you think
about it. So, don't think about it. Stay some
more in the hallway with the rug and the paintings
and your own dashed desires stuffed into your
pocket. And only when your pockets start to drag
you down should you reach for the door, feel
the tickle of lock chambers dropping as you turn
the knob. Take that last deep breath before
you look at this brand-new mountain, before
you say hello again to this unfinished love
that has been waiting, so patiently, for you to arrive.

Forgetting You Is Like a Lion

pawhappy and swatting
at me like I'm a heatwave
mosquito. I try to explain
that you and I are over,
and can I please enjoy my tea?
I offer to add you to my
history or my reflection,
showing up as a frown line
of a single gray hair. But

if forgetting you insists
on being like a lion complete
with jungle crown, years
of sniffing for blood, I might
have to get a weapon. Not

a gun, per se, or a spear, but
something better. Legs that can
outrun a memory or eyes
that can stare down a catbeast,

look into its open cave mouth,
and when it rolls out that long
carpet tongue, I can simply
stand there and yawn back.

After the Movie

I knew you were gone.
I had watched you in the dark theater,
your face ghost white
with the screen's reflection.

That's me up there,
I could hear you think.
Poor lonely sap in the film
and his life sandropping

its way through an hourglass.
You have only so much life,
his leading lady tells him.
I could see you nod

just slightly, at the screen.
Before the movie, you talked about your mother
how her heart is breaking
down in her chest. All the things

she can't do anymore. And your father,
a tired starfish with the *New York Times*. His
life and all the air let out.

After the movie, we went for coffee,
and there was something,
something extra only a trained eye
would see. The slightest movement

of a head, turning away forever.

Bad Enough

how my husband took her
to the river, this young girl
he couldn't leave alone. I saw him
smile wrong at her when she came
by that first time, looking to run errands
because her father broke his back,
and they were going poor. I saw my husband

staring at her breasts,
making me a part of his secret.
What made it worse was how
the papers would tell it, the drowning,
the girl and my husband pulled out
of the nightwater, the used condom
on the riverbank and the empty bottle
of wine she wasn't old enough to drink.

Worse even than that, her father,
who it turns out never broke his back
at all, and would later send me the bill for his daughter's
burial. And not because he was going poor
the way she'd said, but because he had given
up on her, after his wife caught the two of them
in the attic, and left them together forever.
The daughter deciding right then she'd had enough
and started looking for her father in other men.
It became the town secret

that everyone knew. Her father, who had now gone
booze-crazy, and the mother, living hidden
in another town. And the girl, just hours
before meeting my husband that night

primping for their date, maybe
fluffing up her hair, checking her lipstick,
her red mouth pouting and unpouting into
the air like a beautiful, doomed fish.

How the Car was in Neutral

sliding backward, the baby
still in the backseat, and the mother
who would later tell the jury, tell
the judge that she could have sworn
that the car was in park, how she got
out for a second, *a second* to wipe
the birdshit off the windshield. How
she couldn't have known that the scrubbing
would slide the car from behind
her hands. How the wiper blade
would snap as the dinosaur weight
began to build, what she would later
tell the grief counselor was like death
winning an arm wrestle. How all the time, the baby
was strapped in good and tight, never
once crying, not even with her mother
running behind, screaming
into the open-mouthed air. How the car
reached the lip of the cliff that would unhinge
its valleyjaw and swallow the car like a gumdrop,
how there would be that second of pause, of hope
that everything could freeze right there,
but doesn't.

And then, how she would feel
each night after that, lying sleepless next
to her husband, the steady breaths that
snored accusation, his chest going up and down
till she finally shakes him awake, spits out
that the kid wasn't even his, so quit it. How as soon
as the words leave her mouth, she can feel him slip
away, his body behemoth, unstoppable. How
she can hear him padding past the babyless
nursery, and when he does come back it's with

a kitchen knife that he slides down the road
of her throat. How she could see her own life
slipping out from under her, heading towards
the cliff. How she hopes this time, she can make it
pause, make it stop right there. But how, in the end,
once again, all she can do is watch.

We Sit at the Corner Table

because no one needs to see the end
of love. To the untrained eye, we are

romance, a cuddle of arms and shoulders
tucked off to the side, our love bunched

up in the restaurant's elbow. But it's not
an elbow, it's more of a closing fist. The first

time you brought me here, this room
was an open hand, lifelines running every

which way. But now, you pour
a glass of wine, red as a heart stain.

We are silent, because after all this time,
what is there really left to say? You

crunch a crust of bread, I tap a fork
on the wine glass. I used to think that love

went out with a sonic boom, shaking you awake
at 4 a.m., but now I know better. The sound

of dying love is simple. A clatter of dishes,
and the conversation around us

of which we are no longer a part.

III

Something Dead Is Living Here

and it's not just the zombie-me
leftover from your leaving, not
just the woman-shell, the only house
that can still hold in my rickety
bones, my tasteless-as-tap water blood.
No. Something dead is living here, and
not just in my head. It is real as remember,
real as that pocket of times you loved me
that I sewed into the lining of my heart.

The thing that is dead stenches clear
to the house next door. At night, I hear
the neighbors banging the walls for
some kind of relief. I want to tell them
that what is left behind, the dead thing
that lives is just the stinky corpse that is
my future, the future that no matter what
I do wakes up dead each day, takes its
crumbly ass over to the living room couch,
picks up the remote and just chills…

Sometimes the World

pale and icy as it was,
would winterchill us soft-drink style,

freeze us into forgetting about
flight, electricity, breath.

It was as if the sun just stopped,
tired of giving us heat and light.

Find something else to feed you,
it seemed to say. *I shine all day,*

*and you still haven't cleaned up
after your last silly war.*

Meanwhile, gravity pulls at us
needy-child style. Keeps us

from reaching the moon again,
which we could be doing rocketwise

or maybe standing on one another's
shoulders, human-pyramid style.

The Mosquitoes Show Up

after the rain. We are grocery.
Fat oysters with moonpearls
growing inside. We drench ourselves
with bug spray. The mosquitoes
laugh. We hear it as hum.

Nearby, the roses go sunyellow.
The bees will be busy elsewhere
for now. We should be grateful for that.

Ownership

is just for the moment. Everything
has to go back. Even the sky,
all grabby with rain, at some point,
will have to let go.

Each day my life leads my legs
wherever it wants, marches me
to bad decisions and wrong lovers,
as if it had forever. Goes on like the ocean

that keeps drowning itself, wave reaching
over wave like comfort arms, its brief stay
on shore ending with a lunar pull. The same
way that, one day, this minute of me

will tick itself out, my life raining out
of my body, puddling at the edge of the sea,
simple and quick, as if inhaled by the moon.

Anything…Something

What goes into that ellipsis
is the chipping down to specifics.
Block of marble revealing its David.
But what Michelangelo missed
was the small, impossible heartcry,
Wait! I can't let go of this
warmcold marble I am holding!

Centuries pass, and the thought creeps
in that if my own heart is too sculpted
and buffed, standing tall for all to see,
then what would be left for someone
to add? It's human to want to leave
a thumbprint. And besides, my heart

really would do better as unformed David,
stifling in its own marble coffin, rather
than standing out there in the open
for anyone to see, but not to touch.

How it Begins

You watch the leaves burn, turn
to ash and scatter on the road,

swirl like the soft whispers
that trail behind a widow who won't

believe the truth about her gone
husband, even though it had been

etched all along in his distracted face.
You hear the noise the boys make

as they clatter through their teenage
years and shape the weapons they

use to kidnap hearts. You feel the dew
beneath your feet, the grass so green

and new, the sky in morning blue,
the day ahead, a hidden stone with only

a layer of soil waiting to be swept away.

Two Old Sisters

The older was the pretty one,
still keeping the secret about long
achy nights with her sister's husband,
his hand hushed over her breast.
Mornings after, she would want
to confess, but his touch kept her
stupid and too much in love.

The plainer sister knew it
all along. Had lived with it since
twelve years old when the neighbor
boy agreed to kiss her if she'd promise
to put in a good word. She had to accept
that this is how it would always be
and that half was better than none,

better than the lonely life her mother
predicted, leaving her more in the will
to make up for the beauty she didn't
divide. The older sister had her own
stuff. The abortion, the stack of excuses
she cherished like love letters. She used

to wish her beauty away, thinking
it helped in life to be plain. No one
trusted beauty, not even her, knew
it would up and leave someday
just like her lover, just like her
mother, who favored the plainer sister,
leaving her more, after all, in the will.

And what did it matter anyway?
The two old sisters sitting now
by a window. Evened out by age.

The secrets they are still holding
on to, covering them like a shawl.

Grief

is a slow eat
        through the dirt.
The mouth of things opens,
        and you try to hold
on, grasp at the flat marble
        walls, nothing to grab onto.
Meanwhile, underneath, the cracks
        grow wider, and the stony
beach around you is about to fade
        under the wash of sea foam
rushing its way back to shore.

End of the Day

and the sunlight slumps over
the roof, and sleep starts to gather
in your legs, your eyes, and the rooms
fill with vanishing light, and pockets
of the day become part of you, and you
are just another body now, reaching
for night dreams to tell you who you
were, who you are, or who
you will become, and if you ever
do get an answer, you might
believe it was there the entire
time, right in front of you, waiting,
just waiting, for you to stand still.

Doubt

Maybe it's noon, or maybe midnight,
or maybe just 12 o'clock. Maybe your baby
was fathered by lust and not your husband.
Maybe this is all a game. Maybe we are the players,
or the pieces, or the lookers-on who shake their
heads and bring us snacks. Maybe you are the same
amount of alive when you are asleep as when
you are running a marathon. Maybe holding
your breath for a long, long time and then
puffing it out in one big blast really
did start that tornado.

Dogs Know

They know from a rumble
of thunder that a storm
is on its way. They know
from the scent that there's
a chocolate cake two houses down.

Dogs know when there's cancer
or bedbugs or fear.
Dogs know from just a tick
of perfume that there's
another woman.

Dogs know, but they can't tell you.
We are the ones with speech.
Stupid irony. All they can do
is pop up their heads. "Listen,
there's trouble" or "something

has changed." Dogs know
you don't believe them.
That's why they settle back
down to the floor like an unrisen cake
till whatever it is blows over.

Cycle

First, the forests fell.
Trees to the ground

like belly-flop divers,
their leafheads against

the earth, full and green
and useless. Then we turned

the land into parks and yards,
planted lettuce and beans, so we

could pretend we weren't spinning
around on a dying rock. Or that

we weren't just another mother
sending her child off into the world,

holding her breath, waiting for another
forest to burst its head up

through the soil.

Crop Failure

My father looks out the window
at our tired garden, past the cracked-soil
pots lining the deck. All kinds of thoughts
swirl in his head like dustbowl swarms.

He pushes back his breakfast bowl,
heads out to the car, part gas, part
electric, his only nod to the future,
the future without his wife, my mother,
who got swept away last March.

My father brings a basket of store-bought
flowers each day to her grave. Arranges
them to look like they are sprouting there.
Then he waits, patient as a harvest farmer,
the only one for miles whose patch of land
was spared by a freakish rain. But no,

today will be like every other day, him
scooping up yesterday's fallen petals,
pulling the stems just starting to brown,
his knees digging the ground into their own
small graves. Then he will plant the crop

for today, peonies, my mother's favorite.
Standing up, he is hopeful, though deep down
he knows that nothing will grow in this ground
that holds my mother like a dead, remembered seed.

Instead

The seahorse curves and straightens
its tail juts, its horsehead forward.
On land, it wouldn't last a minute
any more than a starfish could twinkle
in the sky. And your chess pieces don't
fool anyone. Kings of no country, bishops
of no church. Just like the guy sitting
across from you, sipping coffee. Deep
down, you know he is holding the place
between your last great love and the next.
But for now, he is a reasonable facsimile.
Strong shoulders and eyes like soft, brown
earth, the kind you might plant a tree in,
let it grow for years until you chop it down,
drag it into the house, strand it up
with tinsel and popcorn. Make it look
as little like a tree as you possibly can.
Knowing that it wouldn't last
a minute outside in the snow.

11:59

when you sleepstumble into the late
night kitchen where all the daytime hum
has dulled down to a drone from the fridge.

In that final moment before midnight,
when hunger wakes you like a lost love,
and you toss for a moment in bed

begging for another chance at one
good night of sleep. But here you are
face to face with need, the spices on the wallrack

eyeing you like a jury. You think in this space
before tomorrow that you shouldn't have to explain
yourself anymore. And anyway, you know deep down

that whatever you are truly searching for will be
tamped down by morning with its cracked eggs
and baconcurl, all of it blending in like milk

swirling into your coffee.

Thirst

We are thin now, hands dry as old wishes.
All we wanted was love but settled for a passing
touch. Inside, too, we are desert. Even for the miles
of blood, oasis of heart. Nothing really is wet
enough to quench the constant need. Each
morning, we wake up drenched in sweat. Tempted
to drink it, lick it off our fingers. Instead, we wring
our empty hands above the kitchen sink. Each day
is a bony crawl on our bellies. Sand-scratched
as we claw our way to evening. And every night
we realize, how exactly the same we have become,
older than our whole lives, younger only than our death.

Things I Didn't Expect

The pink tongues filled with
bad stories. The roll call
of the newly dead. The earth spinning
but us not getting dizzy. Big boats
lifted by the wake of smaller boats.
Telling a joke that nobody gets.
A drop in the bee population.
A man stuck in a well, handclawing
his way up the sides. Black checkers
jumping over red ones. Everyone moving
in different directions. Everyone ending
in exactly the same place.

About the Author

Francine Witte is the author of five poetry chapbooks and two flash fiction chapbooks. A full-length flash fiction chapbook, *Dressed All Wrong for This* has just been published by Bluelight Press as the first-prize winner of their contest. A novella-in-flash *The Way of The Wind* was in the top six manuscripts of the Bath Flash Fiction Contest and was published by Ad Hoc Press. *The Theory of Flesh* is her second full-length poetry collection with Kelsay, *Café Crazy* being the first. Her poem-play, *Love is a Bad Neighborhood,* had a week-long run in New York City, on December 2018. She is the editor of *Flash Boulevard,* a weekly Facebook column on the *Poetrybay blog.* She lives in New York City.

www.ingramcontent.com/pod-product-compliance
Lightning Source LLC
Chambersburg PA
CBHW021024090426
42738CB00007B/900